This coloring Book Belongs To:

....

ALLIGATOR

Bb

BEE

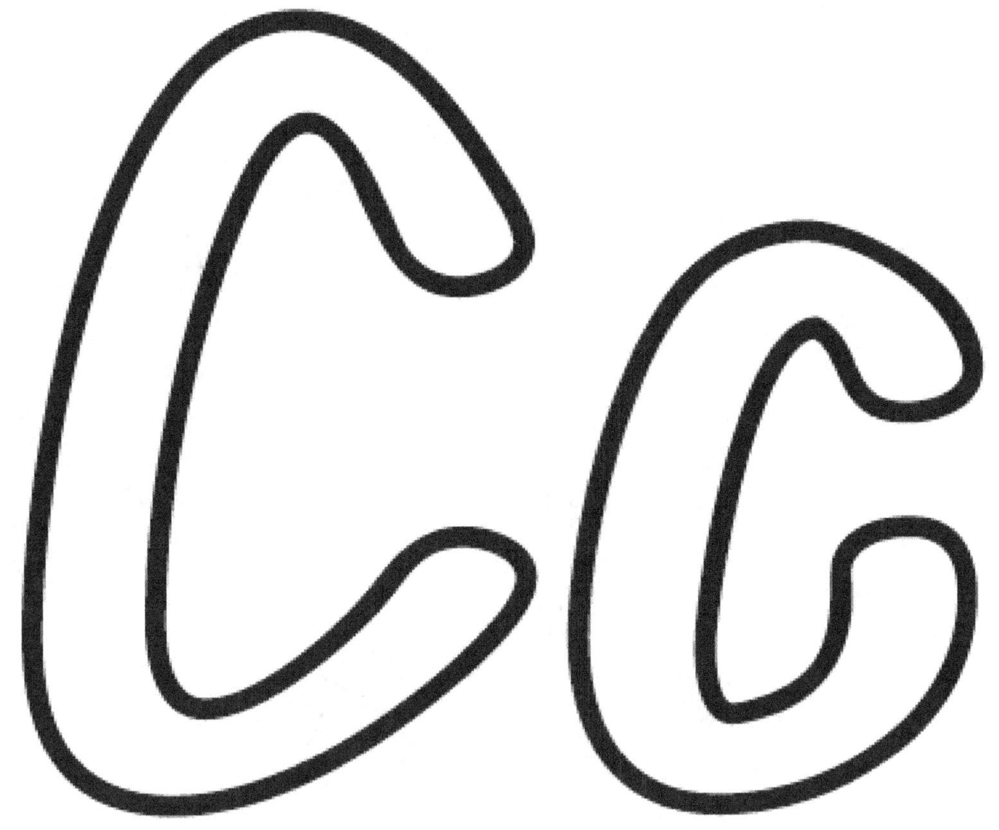

CAT

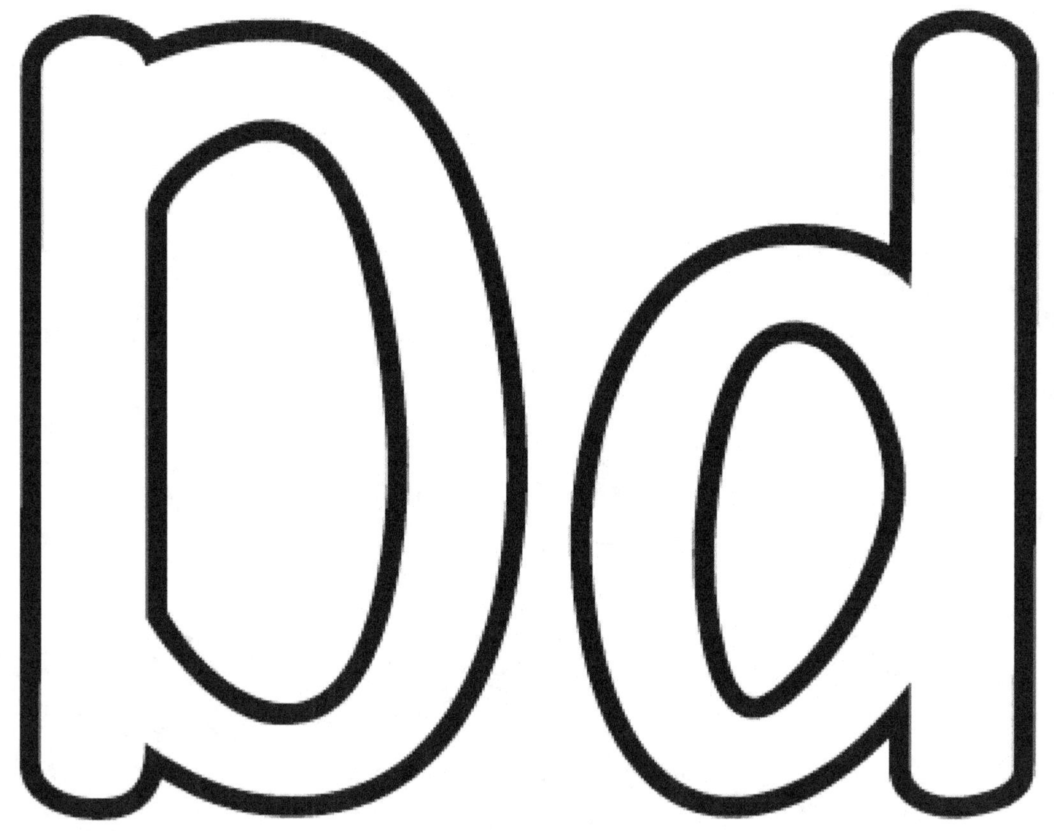

Dd
DOG

ELEPHANT

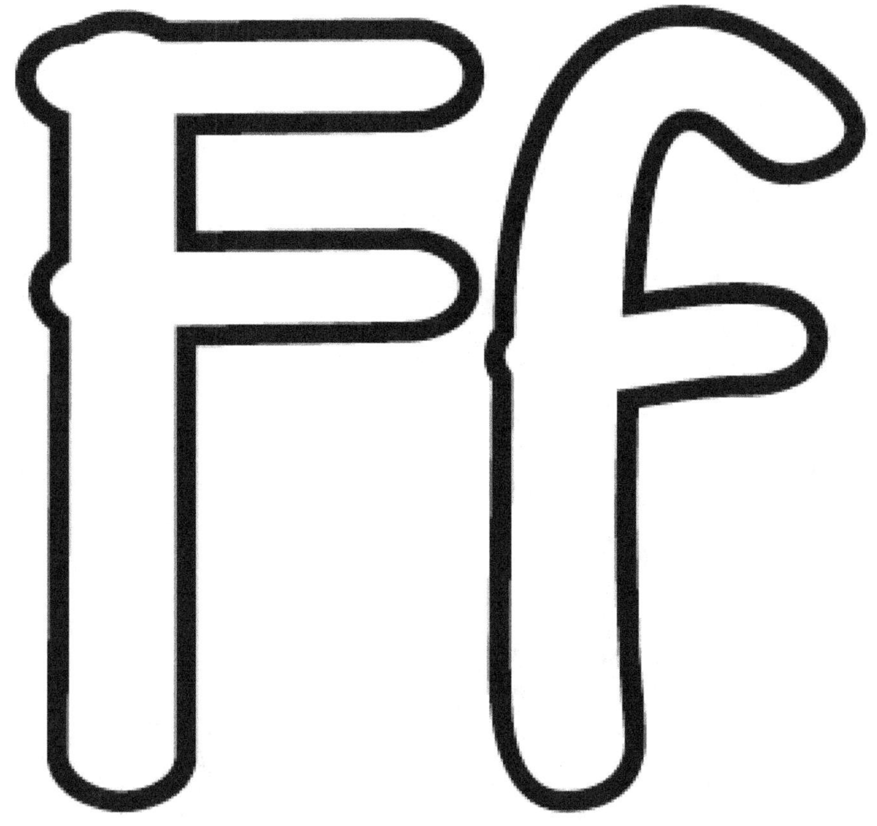

FOX

GIRAFFE

Hh

HIPPO

Ii

IGUANA

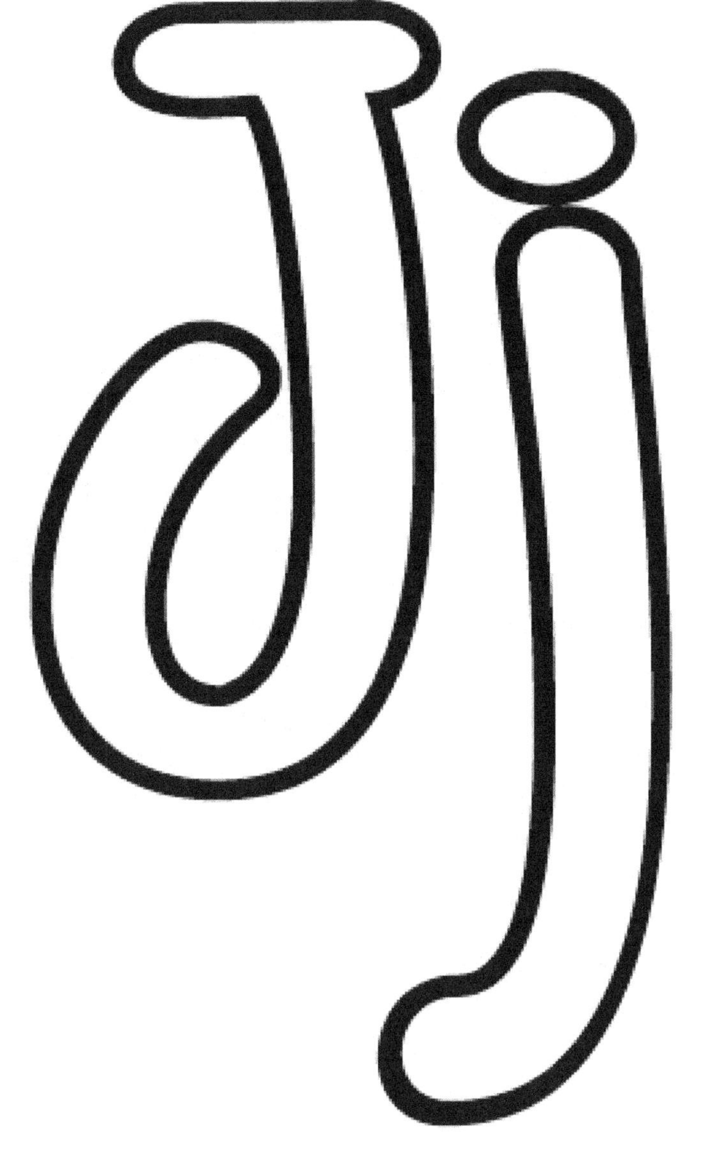

JELLY FISH

KANGAROO

Ll

LION

Mm

MONKEY

NIGHTINGALE

owl

p p

PENGUIN

Q Q
QUAIL

Rr

RACOON

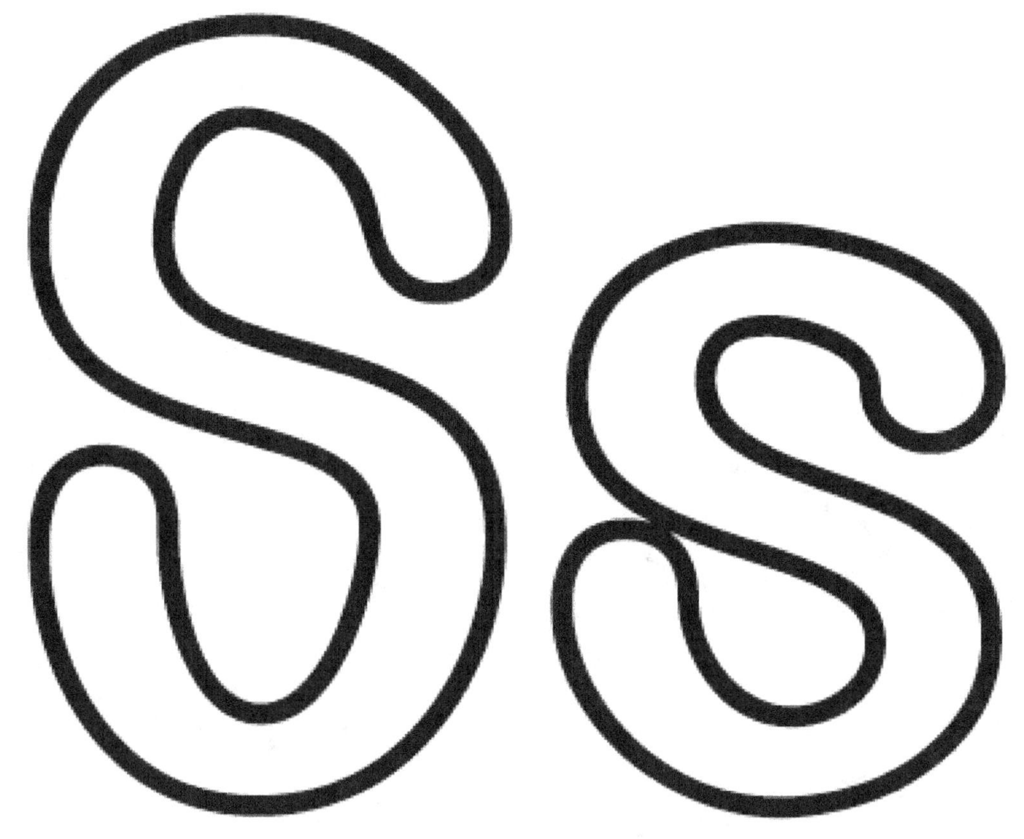

Ss
SEAL

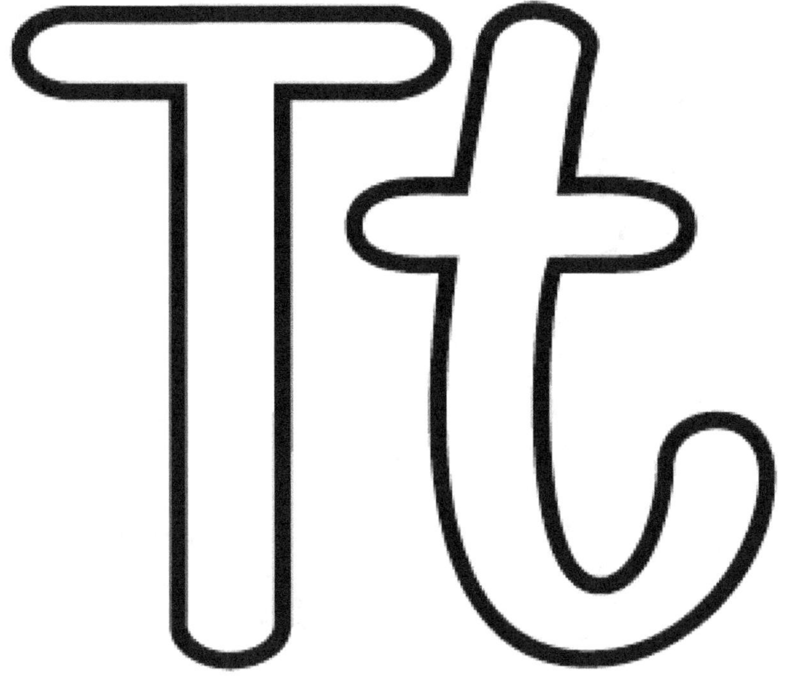

TURTLE

UNICORN

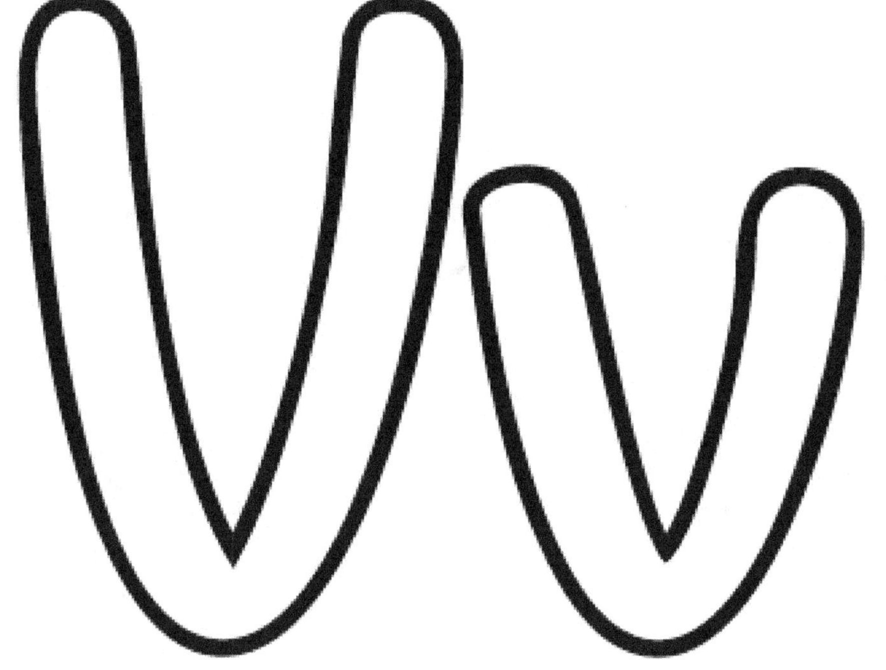

VULTURE

WHALE

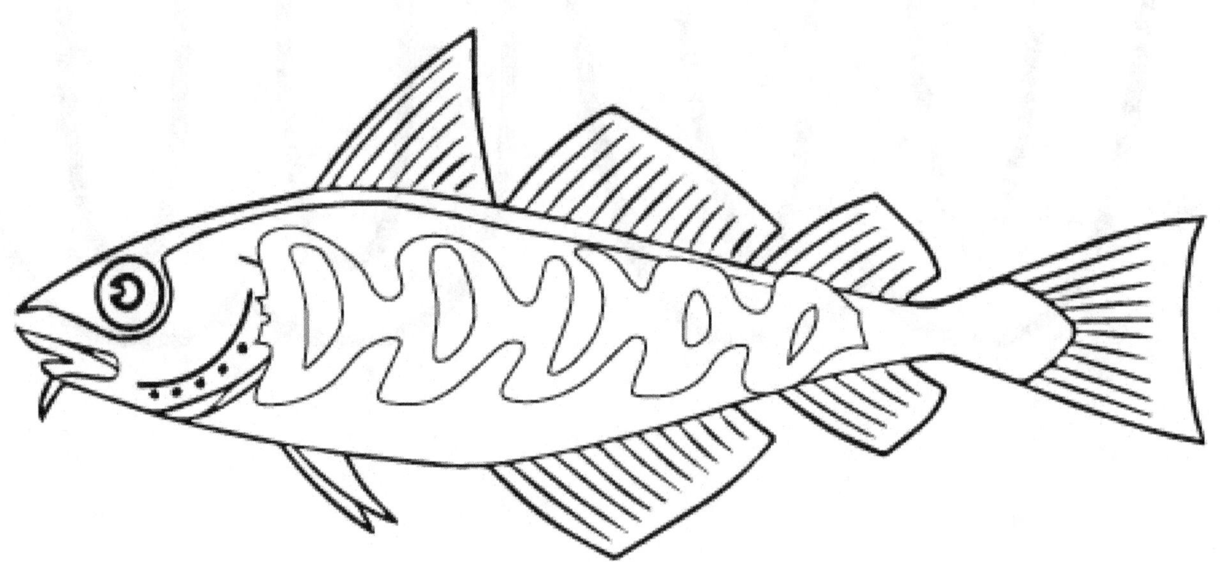

Xx

X-RAY FISH

Yy

YAK

Zz

ZEBRA

Oussa Publisher, 2020

ISBN 9798588168885

https://www.facebook.com/Oussa-Publisher-103909331644015